Lessons We Were Never Taught

Also by Nikesha Elise Williams

Four Women
The Appeal of Ebony Jones
Love Never Fails
Adulting

TED Talks

Pregnancy is Inconvenient — TEDxFSU
Representation Matters — TEDxFSCJ

Lessons We Were Never Taught

Nikesha Elise Williams

Copyright © 2020 by Nikesha Elise Williams

Library of Congress Cataloging-In-Publication Data

Williams, Nikesha Elise.
    Lessons We Were Never Taught/Nikesha Elise Williams

   ISBN 978-1-7335848-5-2

PUBLISHER'S NOTE
Without limiting the rights under copyright reserved above, no part of this publication may be reproduced, stored in or introduced into a retrieval system, or transmitted in any form, or by any means (electronic, mechanical, photocopying, recording or otherwise), without the prior written permission of both the copyright owner and the above publisher of this book.

The scanning, uploading, and distribution of this book via the Internet or via any other means without the permission of the author is illegal and punishable by law. Please purchase only authorized electronic editions, and do not participate in or encourage electronic piracy of copyrighted materials. Your support of the author's rights is appreciated.

*To my future daughter,
and her daughter,
and her daughter . . .
and little black girls full of magic and wonder . . .
may you gather and glean,
all that you need*

to fulfill your soul.

Contents

Ntozake	11
Langston	19
Kingston	24
She.	28
Me.	30
Her.	35
D. W. Donald	40
Nina	50
Beth	58
4:43	67
Molly	72
Bill Robert Harvey	75
Pro-Life?!	83
Mothers of Sorrow	91
A Tribute to Men	99
Malcolm and June	107
Baldwin	114
Mylen	122
Maya	130
Joy	139

"It takes a long time to accept what's been given to you from your past."
— James Baldwin

"It takes people a long time to learn a very little."
— James Baldwin

"We are the ones we've been waiting for."
— June Jordan

Ntozake

Her name means:

She Who Comes With Her Own Things.

Well, here I am.
Here, I stand.
With the name my mama gave me,
and these bags I've been carrying since I was a
baby.

They hold my mommy's stuff.
Which means they hold my grandma's stuff.
Which means they hold my great-great
great-great—
back to the village 400, 500 years before
bondage and enslaved—
grandma's stuff.

This bag . . . is my bloodline.
The line that crossed the sands on the hands of
time.
From beach to beach and shore to shore,
from the door of no return;

From ship to auction,
field to freedom,
reconstruction and setbacks of segregation,

and promises of integration that never came true.

Through civil rights,
and the fight to elect the first great black hope;
that caused tears to tremble down the old guards wrinkled face.
The historic election that made us wonder if
we   were   post   race?

Because if the black man could get to the White House with a sista on his side,
then surely this bag my mama gave me is now a Birken I can show off and carry around with pride.
Until I realized . . .
That,   no matter how soft the leather of my luggage,
it's still meant to hold my life's worth of detritus . . . my dust.
The sins of the mother wrapped up and presented as garbage.

So, now as I try to unpack this bag.
This history born into my anatomy,
the trauma that is as much a part of me as the phenotype provided by my DNA,
I realized I'm surrounded by even more bags I've picked up along the way.

Bags I gathered as I toddled down streets and was patted on the head by well-meaning white folks who have yet to learn that black babies aren't the same as baby ducks you see waddling in your yard begging for bread.

There are no pickaninnies here.
Just little girls who hear the refrain of the women going:

"Close your legs."

"Sit up straight."

"Make good grades."

"Get a good job."

"Find a good man."

"Don't have too many kids."

"Keep yourself together."

"Go to church."

"Worship Mother Earth."

"Curse the man who cheated."

"Learn how to fuck because one day you might need him."

All of that is in these bags
A bag at 3.
A bag at 13.
A bag at 23 and 33.
And there are bags waiting for me at 43 and 53,
63, 73, and 83.

I got bags with no bands.
Bundles with no bills.
My crown has been bought and paid for,
but it's still too far down, in one of these damn
bags, I can't even find it to put it on.
All I have at the ready . . .
is my own version of a crown of thorns.
Piercing my skin,
Causing my blood to flow from my temple, to
my cheeks, to my chin.
Until it dries up in a crimson stain I can't wash
out.

No amount of salvation will help me put down
these bags.
No amount of ritual cleansings will help me
unpack these loads that I have.
This is my stuff.
Can't nobody can just walk off with it.
Make off with it.
Take what I've picked up,
and packed up,
and buried so deep, down inside myself,
that the me I see in the mirror . . .
    I   don't   even   recognize.

Nikesha Elise Williams

The girl with the easy smile and eager eyes . . .
She's gone.

She has lost her glow.
Her shimmer is dim.
Her halo crooked, without polish, and
unvarnished.
She has bruises.
I have bruises.
I have bruises and I can't even see them.
Red, blue-black, purple and ugly;
these here bags carry the seat and the soul of
my suffering.

I have paper cuts, that have turned into gashes,
that have turned into wounds.
Wounds that come from carrying these bags for
far, far too long.
But I can't just put them down;
I can't just bury my bags at wounded knee.
I can't do that to my bags.
Hell, I can't do that to me!

These bags have subsumed pieces and parts of
my body and helped deliver me.
You see . . .
The handles have melted into my skin;
twisted so many times around my wrist that
my outer coating — covered in melanin — has
been severed
               and cut
                           to the bone.

Lessons We Were Never Taught

Weathered through the epidermis to get to the
fire shut up in my bones.
The fire that keeps me going when my bags get
to heavy,
my crown too prickly,
my back too bent,
my shoulders too limp,
And my sighs . . .
too   FULL   of wishin' . . .
that someone had room for me.

A premonition from a clairvoyant someone
who could provide a place for me
                                    and my bags.

These. Are. My. Bags.

My past and my present.
My history and my future.
I can't just put them down.
Because what would the fight, the uphill battle
have been for?
What would all the prayers for strength have
been for, if I ain't got nothing to show?

No.

So, I take my bags with me.
I don't put them down,
I pass them down.
Hand them to my daughter, and her daughter,
and her daughter,

until they have to have mega-mansions, and
super-yachts filled with our bags.

And wherever they go,
whenever they arrive,
their bags will go before them.
All ten thousand making room for them in a
world that piles on more bags, and more bags,
and more bags . . .
without ever offering
                a helping hand.

So, yeah, I'll take this bag and that bag,
your bag and her bag,
because I have room for you,
and I have room for more.

I can take some of your load,
so it's not so much for you to hold.
Because that's what they think.
That because I am strong . . .
There is never a muscle,
         a tendon,
         a synapse,
or an emotion   that ever feels weak.

And so I play into their prank;
assimilate, reclaim and acculturate.
Take back my power and multiply it to the ten
thousand to the infinity of powers of my bags,
because that's what happens when
you reclaim yourself,
and rename yourself,

Lessons We Were Never Taught

She Who Comes With Her Own Things.

No one else knows what makes up your stuff.
They don't know what's in your dreams.
They don't know these are just tricks and
slights of hand.
They don't know you've been cut to the bone.
No one else knows.
No one else knows what you have.
Because you . . .
    Because I . . .

I am the only one who can see these bags.

Nikesha Elise Williams

Langston

I heard her when she said,

"Well, son, I'll tell you:
Life for me ain't been no crystal stair."

My mother was talking to my brother,
and I was waiting in the shadows.
I had disappeared myself into darkness where
I could hear and not see . . .
So I wouldn't be shamed for listening to the
lesson she said wasn't meant for me.

You see . . .
Everything I learned, I learned at my mothers
feet.
And then her knees, and her legs, and her
thighs, until I got tall,
and old enough that she began to worry about
me seeing and doing it all.

Because as far as families go . . . they . . . in
general,
tend to love their sons and raise their
daughters,
and mine was no different.
He got the pretty pep talk about life not being a
crystal stair;

Lessons We Were Never Taught

While all I got was the gritty two bit sound bite
on the best way to keep and please a man.

As if the only thing I'm good for is to lay on
my back in a "V," "H" or "L" shape —
and moan and sigh —
whether or not I feel like it.
Because I've learned. . .
My feelings don't matter.
My desires don't matter.
What I want does not matter . . .
    as long as my kids are happy,
    and my partner is smiling.
    As long as the belly is full and the dick is
    empty.
    As long as my woman duties have been
    fulfilled,
    Who cares   if I'm happy?

                Fulfilled?
                In love?
                Enthralled?
                Overjoyed?
                Or even content?

I've learned that my life is in service to others
as soon as I . . .
                          lay beneath,
                          ride on top,
        or look back over my shoulder at
                              another.

Nikesha Elise Williams

In that moment when my body is penetrated
and ripe for opportunity to be impregnated . . .
It is in *that* moment I've given up my power.
Submitted my life, my goals, my dreams, my
wants, my desires over to someone else.

A woman cannot serve two masters.
She must choose between herself and a
significant other.
So, I learned from my mother how not to
choose me.
Not that she said this explicitly,
but it was implied
implicitly
                                       by her actions.

Her overreaction to my self-indulgence,
what she called, "my selfishness."
She had to beat it out of me.
Yell it out of me.
Spank it out of me.
Drive it out of me with the force reserved for
evil spirits.

She performed an exorcist . . .
. . . to kill
           the indomitable voice of my soul.

But try as she might.
Try as he might.
Try as the world might;
my tenacity has never gone cold.
It may not be the force of the ocean,

but it is not a walled up dam,
because what I also learned from my mother
is . . .
that there are certain times to POP OFF,
and remind people of exactly   who   I
am.

Kindness costs me nothing,
but don't take my kindness for weakness.
Because inside of me there is a longing to put
aside my meekness and roar with rage
after being submissive and subservient just in
the name of appeasement.

I am no longer here to please people.
I will only focus on pleasing myself.
My joy.
    My happy.
        My love.
            My content.
                My peace.
Because my mother didn't tell my brother
about all the times she's been climbing those
hard wooden stairs for nothing.
She didn't reach those landings and turn those
corners for me to turn back,
shrink back,
and not acknowledge the unspoken lesson for
her daughters.
Nooo . . .

Maybe she never said it.
But I understood that I was supposed to get it.

This life for me was going to be what I make it.
And what she couldn't do for herself,
she wanted me to do instead.

That's why she always smiled when she beat me,
and laughed when she scolded me.
Because she knew that by raising me,
the world could never break me.
The lessons she never taught me would never phase me.
And the crystal stair she never reached . . .
Well,
    THAT . . .
                Would be mine for the taking.

Lessons We Were Never Taught

Kingston

We used to play house on the front porch.
Popping gum and gum popping,
pop locking and walking with a twist,
trying to put a lil umph in our hips.
But don't let your mama see it.
'Fore she tell you stop being grown,
or else go pull me a switch.

We played double-dutch on the curb,
digging in potatoes until we got inside the ropes.
Singing as we counted:

>   One, one, one,
>   Two, one oh
>   Two oh,
>   Three oh,
>   Four oh,
>   Five oh,
>   Six oh,
>   Seven oh,
>   Eight oh,
>   Nine.

We counted until our feet tangled,
jumping our hearts out on youthful ankles.
Passing time in the setting sun,

neither booked, busy, or bothered about
any wicked ways that would come.

Butter scotch,
butter cookies,
butter cakes with butter creme frosting were
what our dreams were made of.
We may have had knowledge of fly by bullets
and dope fiends,
crazy crackheads and the imminent sounds of
police;
but that was half a world away on the block,
when anybody's mama or grandmama could
clock you.

"Where you going?"

"Who you think you going with?"

"You better be back before it gets dark
outside."

"Don't be running in and out of my house;
letting all the air out—
running up my light bill.
Who you think I am?
Commonwealth Edison?"

"You better get a thought in your head."

"Use your head for more than a hat rack!"

"Li'l girl I don't eat paper and shit money;

do I look like a money tree to you?"

"You must think I'm, Boo Boo the Fool."

The scolding could come in any colorful variation,
but the aunties just wanted us to get in formation.
Ready and prepared for the world's cold calculating discrimination.

But we were more concerned about the life within our atmosphere.
Our realm of vision was nothing but the six blocks surrounding us —
with little thought to a future or career.

We wanted to play:
    dolls and hand games
    "Rockin' Robin," "Slide," and "Shame."

You go up,
    and you go down,
        Then we'll turn right,
            and you'll turn left.

Okay, here we go:
    "She was rockin' in the tree tops all day long,
    loving and a rocking and a singing that song.
    All the little birdies on Jaybird Street,
    love to hear the robin go tweet tweet

tweet.
Rockin' Robin."

We played until our hands got tired,
and our feet got anxious.
Our bodies so bubbled up with excitement
we put the radio in the window;
just to hear our favorite song, while we played
dance party until the streetlights came on.

Until the boys dropped their balls just before dusk,
to run around in low light to play hide-and-go-seek with us.

We played like this for years.

Until . . .
Games of tag turned into games of touch,
and hide-and-seek became hide-and-go-freak.
We were spinning bottles in basement parties
with black lightbulbs,
because there was no reason to hide,
when everyone in the room knew you could go get it . . .

We didn't play no more.

No . . .
We   Experimented.

Lessons We Were Never Taught

She.

I remember my first kiss.
The time I was pressured into pressing up
against pillow soft lips.

We were playing truth or dare.
I was 13.
He was 14,
eyes green,
skin sallow and pink.
I smelled like Ivory and he like Irish Spring.

We were in one of those basement parties with
the dark and moody incandescent lights.
The door was closed,
and
      the music
             was   LOUD.

We rewound our tapes of the radio
just to hear Jodeci,
and every one in the circle around us
crowded in to see.
They kept their eyes wide open,
but I closed mine
to take in the moment
as I experienced my first kiss;
that was the start of an interracial relationship

Nikesha Elise Williams

After that one kiss I went back for more.
I just couldn't get enough.
My awakened pubescent excitement turned
into French kisses every time I got on and off
the school bus.

And because I was giving into my lust,
that automatically meant we go together . . .
Until,
>   summer break,
>   distance,
>   and no weekend minutes,
>   broke us up.

We lost touch.

Lessons We Were Never Taught

Me.

I remember the first time I was touched.
His hands were warm and sweaty against my skin,
and I bet he could feel the goose pimples rising
as I bubbled   with titillation from within.

Fingertips traveled up my arms,
over my shoulders,
until he reached my chin.
With a slight of his hand,
 and a tilt of my face
our lips met and we connected;
and in the taste of our tongues it no longer
mattered that he was
                my best friend.

We were getting to be grown now,
and that means fumbling through clothes to
figure out what this love making is all about.
He tried to be gentle,
and I tried not to wince with pain,
but we didn't know what we were doing,
just that we no longer wanted to be the same.

We wanted to see the sun,
and the stars,
and the moon floating in each other's eyes;

as we learned which way we needed to move
our hips, legs, and thighs.

In the back of a car
parked under a flickering street light.
In the middle of a twin bed when no parents
were downstairs.
We met when we could as we fell deeper into
each other . . .
Fantasizing about what would happen if we
got caught by my brother.

But we lucked up in our sneaking,
never getting found out when we were
creeping.
In these moments of new excitement
exploring bodily forms
and biblical functions,
we didn't care about what we may have to
sacrifice.

It never occurred to us or even entered our
minds
that one day we would have to separate and
divide.
Because what we can't do alone
we can do together,
and what we can't do without
we can compromise.

Because I love you.
Because you love me.
Because we love being a we.

An us.
A plural pronoun.
One you can daydream
and fantasize with
about a night on the town.

That is . . .

Until your dreams run into your realities,
and you realize they no longer line up with
your vision for everything you thought you'd
be.
You realize you have to make a choice;
stay the course,
or make an adjustment,
and it starts with using your voice.

But . . .

The words get stuck,
and tears fall,
and salt stings in wounds that are not yet there,
from the level of stress you've created within
yourself
      you don't know if you can bear.
All you can remember is how it felt when he
touched you there.

It's not a feeling you want to give up.
Even though . . .
It's incongruent with the message board of
manifested visions you've posted,

Nikesha Elise Williams

and you realize in life you can't have your
bread both buttered and toasted.

You have to sacrifice.
You have to compromise.
You have to devise
      a life out of the shitty decisions you're
      forced to pick.
The future of this lust,
I thought was love,
in the form of the teenaged boy I thought I'd
always be with.

Now, it's time to make your list.
Weigh the pros and the cons;
the good and the bad.
How much it will hurt to leave,
versus how much it will hurt to stay.

And in the end
              you give a good
                          "Goodbye."

A few tears shed.
A few fears bled.
Through the blood of your logic,
the thought process that made you go from
paper checks to direct deposit,
because your heart   is not on loan anymore.

It's back in your body.
Completely full,
and in your possession,

Lessons We Were Never Taught

to do with whatever you desire.
To inspire within yourself
those same feelings you remembered from
your first time . . .
                       now with someone else.
So that you may fall
over,
and over,
and over   again.
And in the end
you can always tell a friend,

"I remember
the first time I fell in love

with him."

Nikesha Elise Williams

Her.

The guttural growl erupted from my groin;
the primal cry of a hurt animal.
I was wounded by his words;
hurt,
and caught off guard.
I thought I had made the best decision at the time . . .
Put us over me
so that we could continue on as a we,
but I'm starting to realize that his discontent,
his disquietude,
has nothing to do with me.

And then   I remember   **She.**

The she I was before I ever met he.
The she who was focused and hell bent on one goal,
      and that never included seeing a state secretary.

The she who never thought she'd see the inside of a room for delivery.
The she who was honest to a fault,
who wielded truth like a sword,
and made best friends with veracity.

Lessons We Were Never Taught

The she that said,

    "I never want to get married."

That's what I told myself.
I'm never getting married.
Because the only marriages I see   have:
Pain.
Sacrifice.
Compromise.
The kinds you unwillingly decide.

I don't want to get married.
That's not for me.

I was even iffy in a relationship,
more like well, maybe.
I never wanted to get married,
didn't want to live a lie.
To be forced to deny myself
                        intrinsically.
The pieces and parts of me only I can see;
my kinks and quirks that take patience to understand,
and yet here I am hitched   to a man.

Married and unhappy,
don't wanna stay,
don't wanna leave;
just want to be alone and find peace.
Want to escape my fears of losing out,
forget to be afraid on the fear of missing out,
of white picket dreams

Nikesha Elise Williams

I never lucid dreamed for me.

Yet here I am
in ever after
unhappily.
With some two-carat bling that means I'm
forever bound
to someone else,
that I belong to someone else,
that I am property of someone else.
The certificate that certifies our contract says
I no longer even belong to myself.
And all I long for is to be she once again,
but now
                  I am **Her.**

Her is wed and with child.
A baby on her hip
and a baby in her belly,
confused about whether or not to terminate the pregnancy.
So that her can get pregnant with herself.
So that her can be filled with she again.
Single again,
back on the block,
to troll the lanes of her mind
                                      again.

But her doesn't want to be she and alone
                                      again.
Going to bed at night by herself
                                      again.

With only her baby's short limbs to keep her warm,
the beating heart and unstank breath of
mother's milk to keep her calm.
The calm she invites
to create a space inside she self
to keep from going insane.
The insanity that whispers to you in the
evening, "Suicide is okay."

She is ready to cross a line.
Her is gassing her up to be cool with no longer
being defined.
And we . . .
We are ready for whatever is on the other side
of this divide.

Ready to see what comes after we detonate the
bomb in our own lives,
pull the pin in our own grenade,
and be damned if we run and hide.

If **She**, if **Her**, if **I**
                become the dust
then scatter me wherever you think is fine.
Put my ashes somewhere my children can't
find.
Tell them only of the happy moments we had
before my soul began to cry,
and my spirit began to die.

Tell them of me before I lost my fight.
Tell them of me of when I had strength to fight.

Tell them of me when I was full of muscular
curve and might.
You know what,
tell them all about **She**   before **She**
              became
          the ended **Me.**

Tell them about her who was full of optimism
and adventure,
but whatever you do don't tell them about me.

Don't tell them about this brokenness before
you.
Don't tell them about what I turned into.
Don't tell them how I transformed into neither
hero or villain,
how I became one of the people in the distance
you forget,
an extra in my own life who didn't think her
time was well spent.
Don't tell them of the me you know as of late.

Tell them of the strong
               She
                  and **Her**
before I was overtaken by these symptoms

of heartbreak.

Lessons We Were Never Taught

D.W. Donald

I wake up in the morning and wonder,
"What's it like to be at the top of the food chain?"
Instead of just being looked at as a descendant
of people who used to work on chain gangs.
Or a member of the gender who's urged to go
back to their homes
                      and be wives
                                  and kitchen slaves

In money,
power,
beauty,
and pay,
I want to know what it's like to always get
your way.
Is it care free?
Is it easy?
Do you get to pursue every flight of fancy?
Because what I've found in my mere existence,
is that when it comes to being black,
and female . . .
      your attitude toward me is consistent.

You love everything about me.
You love everything about me;
                                  except me.

Nikesha Elise Williams

My cares and my desires.
My health and my well-being.
My passion and my pain.
You cannot separate   me   from it
we are one in the same.

My pain is responsible for the birth of my joy,
but you don't want me.
No . . .
You want pieces and parts of me.
You want to cherry pick my skin,
                my nose,
                my eyes,
                my ass,
                my hair,
                my waist . . .
Frankensteining all the things you love until
you have a docile, freaky, training ape.

That's how you see me . . .
like the gorillas at the zoo.
To be awwed and ogled over,
behind see through glass walls that prevent me
from showing off my true power.
Because heaven forbid you see me flex at what
I can do.
Do something better than you.

You on that man shit.
That masculine testosterone shit.
That   I got a dick,
and I got the right to ego trip   shit.

Lessons We Were Never Taught

But, Baby, you came from a vagina.
And the only way your seed continues
is when you come to submit
to the divine within her.

Even God used a woman to birth the Son of Man.
And yet you think because you were made in his image . . .
> it gives you the right to suppress,
> step on her neck to relieve your own stress,
> subjugate and oppress,
> even though
> you want her to keep giving up the sex.

So, you see, I wonder what it's like to be at the top of the food chain?
To be seen as more than who I marry,
and to get more than what I negotiate.
To be valued at my infinite worth,
instead of being forced to show, and prove, and demonstrate.

The Bible says I can't serve God and money,
but I ain't got two dollars
> two quarters
> two nickels
> or two pennies,
and I don't think that shit is funny.

God gave the Ten Commandments.
Jesus had two.

Nicky and Biggie had The Crack Commandments,
let me hip you to the money few.

Equal pay for equal work.
I got 68 cents to your whole buck.
According to you I should just be happy to be here . . .
and grateful that I'm even breathing this rarified air.
Happy to just be in the room where decisions are made,
instead of having a seat at the table and being an actual catalyst for change.

It's the story they sell
to get us in the door;
when their success depends on our presence more and more.
To meet their quotas and pretend like they believe in diversity.
Counting the new bodies like,
    "I got a black,
        a woman,
            a Hispanic,
        and a LGBT."

We are nothing more than check marks in a box
to their global dominance.
The reason they hold all the wealth in the world,
and we're stuck struggling in the ninety-nine percent.

Lessons We Were Never Taught

The reason the boys club will never be broken,
and no matter how high on the corporate
ladder we climb we'll always be a token.
Whether as President
or even in a pulpit,
we are seen as nothing more than a nuisance,
and our fuel   to feed   our desire
is seen   as mere   pretension.

No matter how many equal rights for which
we fight,
the three-strand cord of male tradition
never cowers in the face of our ambition.
And at the tiniest semblance of a threat,
debate then devolves into reducing us to the
parts of our sex.
And at worse we're othered to be outsiders in
some radical,
      political,
   or ideological sect.

It's the reason Twitter fingers turn into trigger
fingers   aiming,
        pointing,
        blasting,
those whom they cannot control.
The women whose bodies they don't own,
the ones whose pussies they can't grab,
and The Squad who defiantly stands
against angry mob mentality chants of,
     "SEND.   HER.   BACK."

Nikesha Elise Williams

So, you see, I wonder what it's like to be at the
top of the food chain?
Instead of running a rat race,
riding a hamster wheel,
crossing and recrossing a bridge to nowhere;
    a place without a name.

We are last hired, and first fired.
Elected and then rejected,
forced to figure out work-life balance,
while you get an applause for picking up your
drawls . . .   our sacrifice is expected.

Always told to put off the self to build up the
us.
Told that we can't handle the equality of
responsibility,
and the word individuality has no place in our
vocabulary.
We can't afford to find the laze in a day to sit
around and dream,
because there's a steady call of the alarm;
        the false belief that work will set
        us free.
That our education is the key
to elevation,
and not the ideas we conceive.
The negativity becomes our own self-fulfilling
prophecy.

We believe the lies:

Dreaming	is for rich people while we gotta go to work.
Dreaming	is for white people who dry clean their sheets and shirts.
Dreaming	is for people with three college degrees paid out of a trust fund.
Dreaming	is for those content to go nowhere bar none.
Dreaming	is for those whose incendiary greed knows no shame.
Dreaming	is for the jailed, committed, or straight up homeless walking around insane.

So, still, I wonder what it's like to be at the top of the food chain?
To sit back and see the chaos of the world's people below, and not give a damn about any of them . . .
        not even the ones who share my name?
But that will probably never be me;
to have a hardened calloused heart held up by systemic systems of patriarchal inequality.

Nikesha Elise Williams

It is my gift to find the groundswell support in
the openly contrary.
To build from the basement until my
movement is revolutionary.
To not be discouraged by a lack of dollars or
cents.
          Because   with
      An army of words
      A quiver of nouns
      And a magazine of verbs
I can move the needle,
and frustrate the clowns.
      Use adjectives to upset the
      administration,
until the harmful policies are permanently
reversed,
thanks to impeachment and exile to a less than
beauteous vacation.

Then the men and women beside me will see
      beyond our sex or sects,
and that reverie in which we believe
      is the only thing that's relevant.

On that day, I will no longer have to wonder
what it's like to be at the top of the food chain,
because the wheel will be broken,
      the ladder structure busted,
      the invite to the table rescinded,
      the injustices written into our laws
          amended.

Lessons We Were Never Taught

No longer will I have to wonder about what
you see when you look at me.
What lies you will tell to keep me from
indulging my hopeful fantasies.
Because at the very least, and without a
shadow of a doubt,
I will know that
Dreaming   is for me.

I will know that higher learning is available,
elevation is possible,
money is no object,
and a secured equal future is tangible.

That I am seen,
and not just something to see.
My stature revered and respected
as much as my beauty.
My pieces and parts are better in tandem to
create a whole picture,
and my differences are what make us better.
My otherness is an asset.
I am no longer a token,
                          but a national treasure.

My unique perspective comes not just from my
adversity,
and my joy, my passion, desires, and cares all
add to the tapestry.
There is no longer a dirty word called diversity
because we've deadened the narration;
and killed the fabrications.

Nikesha Elise Williams

We are now gathered together in an artistic convocation.
And we only stand on the truth
                        that first and foremost
                                      We begat
          the birth of this nation.

Lessons We Were Never Taught

Nina

Mammy.
Fat, black and nappy.
Aunt Jemima in a head scarf.
Dark.
Round and wide.
Quick to tan the hide.
She is Big Mama, Grandma, Grandmama,
Mama, and Mo-Mo.
Everybody's Aunt Sarah.

Her children are her children, and your
children are her children, and their children are
her children . . .
That she calls from down the block, up the
block, and down to the corner.
Little Jack Horner's plus their serving jigaboos
and jungle bunnies.

Saturnine and asexual, used to breed and bear.
Never a heart to share.
No man, no love, no splits, and no tips . . .
Just;
     baby-making hips,
That produce kids, and more kids, and more
kids
to nurse (even if they're not hers)
                              and discipline.

Ridden by whips all across her back.
Her resilience.
Her strength.
Envious of everyone and no one.
The backbone.

Raised on neckbones.
Cooking up creole gumbo and dirty south chitlins,
over a big pot that she loves a lot
with a wide smile and a big ol' laugh to hide the fact
that she too
          is
                  #metoo.

Welfare Queen.
Queen of the ghetto.
The hood chick.
The ride or die bitch.
Hard to the core, holding you down forever more.

Every boy's girlfriend, but never their heart.
Every boy's bust down, but never their heart.
Every boy's first, but never their heart.

So, she found love between her legs and birthed one, two, three, four, five, six, seven mini me's trained up to beg.
For a handout instead of a hand up.
For boots instead of bootstraps.

Lessons We Were Never Taught

Taking advantage of every government thing.
Education.
Breakfast and lunch.
Free and reduced prices.
Teachers that judge by a hunch.
They think they're saints in the hood,
providing attention when the mama is working
at places they can't even mention.
Making ends meet, because it ain't trickin' if
you got it.
Smiling her smile and using her ways
to pay
rent, daycare, lights, gas, water and cable.
Bills, bills, bills.
"Can she even pay her bills?"

But nobody asks what keeps her going still,
because she's just
the used up and ran through,
broke down and beat up hood chick.
The one everybody forgot had so much
promise;
so much talent.
She got caught up, steady, and gum popping
and acting fool,
that nobody remembers the little girl
before
        she was the
                #metoo.

Sapphire,
with a burning desire to succeed.
She wakes up and breathes,

and eats ambition for breakfast,
consumes corporate ladders for lunch.
and dines on mergers and acquisitions for dinner;
until she never has to worry about living off a pension.

She's after more money than a li'l bit.
With no pedigree, but heavily degreed
she is black, bad, and bougie.
Saffronia, not your Sweet thing.
Cunning, conniving, backstabbing and calculating.
Making moves, snatching wigs, and taking names.
Not a chick.
Not a bitch.
She's a BOSS.
But still vulnerable,
but she'll never let them see it.

"Never let 'em see you sweat."

A motto for many,
mastered by some,
a life practice   by one.
A survivor not a victim.
She doesn't get angry.
She doesn't get even.
She gets everything.
Even if it means playing dirty with a devil
who wants nothing more
than to make her scream,

Lessons We Were Never Taught

Knock her back.
Check her mate.
Cock block the next notch on her vision board.
Be the belted noose around her dreams and goals.
Take her down a peg or two,
until she remembers, but never says.
Cries but never admits.
Smiles a lie but never confesses.
Denies until *it* becomes her truth,
That she too
        had a moment
                when she was
                        a #metoo.

Gather around children,
Jezebel's got a story to tell.
About her wiles and her tricks.
The lick of her lips,
the weight of her hips,
her spans and her rise,
because thick thighs save lives.

No frills, a cheap thrill, a high pitched shrill
after a romp in the sheets.
A quickie in heat.
Never seeing anything more than ass and tits.
Not a person, just a thing,
An object of gratification.
Pleasure personification.
Wet and ready,
rocking,

and rolling steady.
Sex, sex, and more sex to cover what sex
doesn't conceal.
Only seen as a delicious meal.
A feast for a misfit, masquerading as a King,
who inserted himself into her being.
Taking her power, pretending she was the one
really in control.

She is beautiful and bold.
Red lips.
Eyes lined black as coal.
Feather lashes and Indian hair inviting the
stares,
but never cares to share,
      what happened to her.

What makes her this way?
A loose wayward woman.
Perceived as promiscuous.
Hottentot Venus,
descended from another Sarah,
a forbear of Peaches . . .
Whose Georgia Peach is always ripe
and ready to bite.
Dipped in cinnamon
and ready to bend to the whims of the
uncouth.
Tell her story
that started in her youth.
It started
   with a
      #metoo.

Lessons We Were Never Taught

Queen.
Come thru, Honey.
Yaaaasss, Chile.
Weeeeerrrrkkkkkkk.

Talk about a glow up.
Boss.
Bad and bougie.
You are fiiiiiieeeeeerrrrrccccccceeeeeee!

Hair is laid.
Edges slayed.
Eyebrows on fleek.
It's all about the contour and conditioner.

Curls poppin'.
Melanin magnificent.
#Blackgirlmagic
Twirl for the Gawds.
You better stroll in the them heels.

I see you sista friend.
Sista girl.
Sista circle.
Group chat confidantes.
#Squad
#Goals
Coming through with the crew.

No new friends.
We taking over.
It's what we do.

Nikesha Elise Williams

Fuck your casting couch.
We're about business.
Not that bullshit #metoo.
Come thru.

Lessons We Were Never Taught

Beth

I said, "Yes."
And then, "I do."
But before all that he asked me if I liked
football, and I said, "Me too."

I said I liked football and beer
    when I really like wine.
I said I liked to stay in and cook
    when I prefer to be wined and dined.
I said I wanted three kids
    when I never wanted any.
I said, "Yes," to everything he did;
    because when it comes to good men,
    I wasn't seeing many.

And we lived our lives like this:
Him suggesting and me agreeing
Him improvving and me playing a steady tune
to keep time.
I am the melody and he is the rhyme.
I am the hook and he is the lyric.
He is the scat and I am the constant metric.

The measure of his metronome.
His ticks and his tocks.
While he goes wild,

I make sure he always comes home to folded socks,
and drawls,
and pressed shirts and pants.
While I settle for starched clothes in the dryer,
because if I'm being honest,
    I never really did like to iron.

But we were good we two:
On this love thang.
This marriage thang.
Hell, we had even managed to take hold and capture the American dream.
We are perfect.
We are ideal.
Three kids.
Big house.
Good jobs.
Good sex.
    At least that's what I told my friends

We go to church on Sundays,
and on dates once a month.
We play hooky from the kids
sneaking around like we are still teens.
But if I'm being honest,
    Sometimes I want to play hooky from him.
    From them.
But I know if I say that out loud,
it's going to come across as kinda mean.

I am bent.

Lessons We Were Never Taught

I am permanently bent.
Like an unraveled paper clip,
bent like a boomerang.
Always coming back to him.
Always coming back to them.
Always saying, "Yes."
Instead of saying, "No."
Ignoring the slow erosion of my soul.
The desperation in my spirit to return to what I
once was before I get kinda old,
and comfortable.
And that's when I ran into my own non-
negotiable.

That's when I ran smack dab into me.
I ran into my own memories.
And I started to explore the inferences of my
own remembrances;
the original dreams I let die.
the goals that never got a deadline,
Because I allowed myself to be
    Subsumed   by him.
        Swallowed.
            Consumed
                Ingested.
                    Digested.
                        Subdued
                            by him.

If he set the box,
then I willingly got in;
closed the flaps,
and taped myself shut.

If he produced the muzzle,
then I was the obedient mutt;
muting my bark
with only a leather bit to sink my bite.

If he opened the cell to my solitary
confinement,
I didn't protest,
even if I wasn't a suspect in the jail fight.

He didn't have to lead the witness.
I incriminated myself.
I submitted to his will myself.
I was obedient by choice.
Crucifying my flesh at the very sound of his voice.
I died on his hillside,
and forgot I even had pride.
Or dignity.
Or ego.
Or any type of anything.
Be it pompous circumstance, or bombast
braggadocio.

I forgot me   to uplift him.
I ignored me   to support us.
Because two are better than one,
And we were a united front.

Even though . . .
I became more of his tether.
The metaphoric shadow people who live life
without agency of their own.
I gave up my agency,

because I thought it was for the greater good.

I reduced myself,
and dimmed my light.
Did more and more
until I barely had a spark
on less than a splint to light.

But somewhere inside that cell.
Somewhere inside the blue-black darkness of
my box.
Somehow, between the straps of my muzzle,
I began to remember that
my first love wasn't a man.
No.
My first love   was my mind.
Singing,
    dancing,
        acting,
            drawing,
                writing,
                    painting,
                        counting,
                    figuring,
              really
            basically
        doing
      anything
I could
find.

But somewhere along the line I either learned,
or I overheard,

that it's supposed to be:
>God.
>My spouse.
>My children.

And never stopped,
never bothered to question,

"Well, where the hell am I?"

No, I took on this role willingly.
Accepted the title of wife complicitly.
Because I bought into the belief that
>if I live alone,
>if I dream alone

Then surely, I will live a life of scarcity.
Without a man to fill me up,
to take up space
to be the completed piece to my whole puzzle,
I would live a life of lack,
and nothing truly fulfilling
could ever take that 250-pound place.

I committed to be a bride, not a boss,
I committed to the amement of the we
agreement, even if that meant . . .
He would be elevated over the goal focused
she at the center of my intent.
I accepted these burdens in the checked box of marriage,
because what I find stifling, some see as an accomplishment.

And I can't even front like I don't reap benefits.

Lessons We Were Never Taught

Shared finances and bigger tax refunds.
A warm body in my bed.
Affection and attention.
Compassionate companionship.
And never a lack of someone to call me out on
my shit   in the name of an intervention.

But I need more than money and a good lay;
more than someone to fight the boogey man at
the bottom of the stairs.
I need more than a mirror for my feelings.
I think what I need is the one thing he can't
provide.
I need the one thing he can't give, take, or hide.
I thought I needed him to abide in my I
the way I did in him.
But what I need cannot come from a her,
                           or him,
                           an us,
                           or them.

What I need is what they don't tell you is still a
requirement of marriage.
When you are blessed into the sacrament,
and ordained as a more perfect union they tell
you,
"Die to yourself.
Baptize your body and be made anew in
name."
The last one you add or change,
is only one of the sacrifices of self you are told
to make.

Nikesha Elise Williams

It is the first bend of many,
until you bend, and you bend, and you bend,
and you damn near break.
Until you're permanently bent like me.
A boomerang that always returns,
    No matter how much the heart yearns.
    No matter how fast the legs beat.
    No matter how fast the arms pump,
I always return
               to my default setting.
Where the last thing everyone is betting is that
I leave.
Because, even though I've figure it out.
Even though I've stepped outside the box,
taken off the muzzle,
earned release from my cell,
and untethered myself from my leash.
I am still bound.
The figurative slave, who though emancipated,
doesn't know how to be free.

Marriage may have not been my goal, but it is
now mine until death bid us part in eternity.
Because,
even though I know what I do and don't need;
my life is to wrapped up
to plot a course to flee.
So, I suppose I can't oppose vehemently
all that's worked out for me
and what my life's turned out to be.
I can give up wishin' and pipe-dreamin' about
what I say I still believe.

Lessons We Were Never Taught

Unless I plan to act on the one thing I realized I need.

More than anything,
more than air,
      breath,
           life,
                or money.
What I need is . . .
Is to finally . . .
Once and for all . . .

Choose me.

Nikesha Elise Williams

4:43

I saw him when he walked in,
but he didn't know I was watching.
Watching his stride.
His gait of confidence.
His gallop of indifference,
and his zest that he had made
hips, legs, and feet move
from side to side.

He didn't know that I knew.
Knew his secrets before he lied.
Knew his troubles even though he never cried.
Knew his struggles even though I never spied.
He didn't know that my empathy gave me insight,
and my high emotional plane a path
to prophetic dream on my behalf.

It was time my subconscious advocated for the lucid me.
That my inner visions cut through my
blockades, barriers, and dimensions
I used to keep me   from me.
Basically,
It was high time that I talked to the woman in the mirror.
Confronted her in a heart to heart.

Lessons We Were Never Taught

Not to tear down or beat up,
but to ask her why she put up with so much.
Why she relegated her love to a simpleton,
a basic pick me,
when the divine within her
destined her to be more than mediocrity.

I confronted her,
and this is what she said to me,

"I want to live a life in the minute of 4:43.
Instead of listening to a song hearing his apologies,
wishing they were your words to me.
When I think about what inspires me,
the first two names that come to mind are Jesus and Jay-Z.
The God who saved my soul,
and the man who learned how not to mess up
his marriage to his wife, Queen Bey."

But I shouldn't have to be Beyoncé or Halle Berry to be your queen.
Shouldn't have to be light skinned, and
redbone pretty to be your dream.
I should be enough as I am.
As strong as I am.
As pretty, or even as ugly as I am.
As smart, or even as dumb as I am.
Because instead of pacifying patriarchy by
smiling at white women,
you could be pouring back into me what I so
freely give to you.

But you rather do for others what you won't
do for you.
Seeking validation
outside of your committed obligations;
because you're too scared
to fight to love
someone who is uniquely qualified,
and capable to handle your internal historical
complications.

You like 'em black, brown, yellow, Puerto
Rican, and Haitian.
Flying the flags.
Learning the dance.
Eating the food
>   to make sure none of your other girls
>   know,
>   *This* is all a ruse.
That you're playing a game,
wearing a mask,
running from the one woman
who loves you enough
to make you confront your past.

You said, "It was one indiscretion."

One tip off my block.
But be it one or 100, I'm still the one who gets
whispered about.
In church parking lots, and grocery stores.
In group texts, and WhatsApp threads.
I'm always the subject of conversation,
even when you're in somebody else's bed.

Lessons We Were Never Taught

How many times do I have to cry for you to
see you are the source of my tears?
You are the cause of all of my fears.
Where once I esteemed myself,
but now all that's been diminished because of
you and our years;
together in each other's lives
sharing space and love lies.

I am haunted by the image of what we used to
be.
What we could be.
But there's no point in praying for a blissful
future,
when behind us we've got so much fucked up
history.

The hurt and pain you want me to forgive,
but I don't think I could live
with myself
being addicted to you.
Codependent on you.
Attached to your view.
When I've never even tried to figure out what I
truly like.

Outside the realm of us and we
there is a life of possibility,
and maybe
not just the tired old trope.
Stand by your man,
take the rope
and hang yourself on his every word.

The nouns, verbs, and adverbs that drip from his lips.
The pejoratives, participles, and prepositions that agitate the adjectives that won't let me defend the indefensible.

I can no longer sift through this rift looking for closure to knit our souls back together.
Soul mates or soul ties
pick whatever words you need to describe why I had to leave with high tide forming in my eyes.

Because despite his infidelity,
and the tarnish to my own integrity,
I learned that every time I took him back,
turned my head and let it slide,
I was the one who compromised my own pride.
So, I took the responsibility,
and realized that as I long as I continued to allow his behavior,
then I too, was cheating on me.

So, I left.

And this isn't a good goodbye.

Molly

She said, "Molly, you in danger girl.
From a hard poke
that you love to choke,
but you rushed in too fast . . ."
Those are the words she spoke.

She said, "Remember what Lauryn said,
that you are a rose.
You are a gem.
You're more than that little trim you give to him.
You're more than your cakes.
More than the birthday drive-by and then flake.
You're more deserving of his time.
Worth more than a cheap date,
or for him to love you down
and then roll, bounce, skate."

She said, "You're worth more.
More of his time,
and his money,
because if he wants to keep getting your good honey
he gotta stop acting hella funny.
Funny about who you talk to.
Funny about who you text.

Funny about how you fit your ass in that body con dress."

She said, "It shouldn't matter about your Facebook,
because it's him that gets your orgasm look.
It shouldn't matter about your IG or who you Snap,
because he sees you in fighting form when you can always snap, clap and trap back."

She said, "He should uplift you in your mind and body.
Fulfill you wholly,
not piece by piece thinking it will bring you peace.
He should want to see you succeed,
Because finding what brings you joy will set you free.
He should trust you with all of his feels,
Even when he thinks it looks like he's bitching up all you see is real."

"He should want to see the capacity of God's capability manifested in you,
because when you keep the Most High at the Head, you don't have to ask, "Who you following, Boo?
He should be able to lead you in prayer if he wants to lead you in life.
Want you to be his side chick, his girlfriend, his baby mama, and his wife."

Lessons We Were Never Taught

She said, "Your tears should be about fears,
and not that he might forsake you for his
career."

She said, "You are worthy."

She said, "You are deserving."

She said, "You add value;
an upgrade.
Like a smooth low-cut fade
with a barber's brand-new straight edge
blade."

She said, "You should be more than open —
like iced oatmeal cookies.
More than a dick stop on his road to nookie."

She said, "You're pretty and perfect in all of
your ways.
Your flaws and all give you storied experience
for days."

She said.
She said.
She said.
She said.

I said a whole lot,
and it started hurting my head . . .

So that's when I got in the bed.

Nikesha Elise Williams

Bill Robert Harvey

The boogey man is real y'all.
But he ain't no boogey,
not a spook,
he ain't no haint.
But he's real y'all.

In the form of: My uncle.
               My cousin,
               My brother,
               My father,
               My best friend . . .

From down the block and around the corner
who said, "We was just playing."
             "I'll show you mine, if you show me
             yours."
             "You can touch mine, if I can touch
             yours."

Grooming me and my sister for a life of
confusion.
Cooing me into doing things my little body
wasn't used to.
Turning me out to turn tricks so that by the
time I'm an adult,
I disassociate myself from my body that does
what it wants   without me feeling at all.

Lessons We Were Never Taught

So numb and liqued up,
          drugged up,
         beat up,
that the niggas beating the pussy up
for a quick fix
from a faceless bitch
don't even register.

The boogey man is real y'all.

And I'm not just talking about incest;
                            but access.
The lights and fame, glitz and glamour,
for those to whom the world has never said,
"No."
The ones who have worldly riches and the
trappings of celebrity,
and no I'm not just talking about R. Kelly.
Or whatever man or woman you want to fill in
the blank that makes a sport out of busting
cherries.

It's the faceless men and enabling women.
The ones whose job it is to accommodate,
to facilitate,
to regulate the good girls from the groupies.
The ones trying to get on,
from the ones just throwing a li'l coochie.

And, yeah, sometimes they can be one in the same;
which is why I guess the victim always gets the blame.

"She was asking for it."

"She wanted it."

"You know shorty's a freak!"

"Why else would she wear that dress?
Buy that shirt?"
Hike up that skirt?"
If she wasn't asking for it.
Begging for it.
Damn near pleading for daddy's dick to punch
through her womb's nerves,
and give her what I deserve."

So, she takes what she's given.
Silenced into submission.
Repeatedly raped for a living.
Getting a tip,
while her pimp gets the whole band to traffic
more chicks,
but y'all ain't listening.
Y'all don't see.
Even though I keep telling you . . .

The boogey man is real y'all.

You don't see him?
Standing there.
Looking.
Lingering.
Lurking.
Lusting.

Twirling his tongue on his lips,
waiting for the most vulnerable sis to
approach.
The one on whom he can smell weakness from
her pheromones;
the scent that gives off
how well she can get him off
if he just says she's pretty.

But all he wants to do is get her name;
and maybe her number.
Take her home so she can't meet his mama.
But her eyes are so tinted from the taint of fear,
the false evidence appearing real,
that she winces and dismisses the slightest
chance he may be   true love.

                Because

The last man who said he loved her was a
monster.
The girl she thought was her friend was in on
the scheme and sent to watch her.
Because there's nothing like the oppressed
being installed as the overseer —
to feel like they're moving up in the hierarchy.
Even though, they're reinforcing the system of
their own subjugation.

This is not meant to be some grand education.
Just a little information to pass along
so we can realize when we have become
guinea pigs being tested on

with propaganda and indoctrination.
The oldest business in the game is not a company,
but a source of bodily invasion.
The inhabiting of a part to conquer the whole.
The giving of a little piece to get the whole damn load.

The source of divine essence for some,
is nothing more than a conquest for others.
Taking the gift and the joy of mothers
and turning it into their pain,
their torment and their shame.
Making them wake up wishing they had been born a boy,
with an indiscriminately masculine name.

But the secret is:
        Boys aren't safe either.
Coming into this world male is not a reputable security feature.
Just because the genome in your chromosome got a "Y,"
doesn't mean you can't end up the the li'l piece
on some predatory man or woman's side.

The boogey man is real y'all.

And so is the fear of the unknown.
The shadow lurking in the alley.
Never reaching the mountain peak of your goals
just staying in the valley.

Lessons We Were Never Taught

There is the fear of police lights and race riots.
The fear of being found out.
The fear of failing.
The fear of a random hand on your shoulder
that could change the rest of your whole life course;
from good to bad, or from bad to worse.
There are fears galore.

I'm not here to tell you that your fear is unfounded,
to pile on top of the people who tell you,
"Get over it."
Not knowing they've taken your fear and
made it compounded.

I'm just here to shed some light.
Talk about a fear that has become reality,
but is rarely spoken.
Because the victims if they escape
are so broken
they feel their story is not fit to be told.
Because, who in the hell would advocate for 'em?

But wherever there is darkness there will
eventually be light.
Which means wherever your boogeyman lurks
. . .
those fears he inhabits and represents
will be forced to take flight.
The man behind the mask has no choice
but to be revealed.
The woman telling you to get over your shit —

you hope —
will never know Biblically how you feel.

The boogeyman that lives inside of us
is just as real
as the one outside our bodies.
The one ready to use sex to prey on our
insecurities,
is no worse than the one who is the sickest of
sycophants,
who makes a handicap out of our
vulnerabilities.

Our doppelgängers we face every day.
The visage in the mirror that always gets his or
her own way.
So, just as we should beware of the boogey
man under our bed,
> stairs,
> or on the stage.
> Around the corner,
> or offering up a raise;

we should be aware of the one that lives inside.
The one we create that feasts on our heart's
desires.

The one that keeps us bound and in chains.
Trafficking in disappointments.
Prostituting in failures.
Tricking in hopelessness.
And hoeing in too numb to feel abuse
to see the tides of change.

Lessons We Were Never Taught

The boogey man is real y'all
    even if he seems kind.

The boogeyman is real y'all
    even if he can't be defined.

The boogeyman is real y'all
    when he comes to wine and dine.

The boogeyman is real y'all
    when he holds you at arm's length
    and says,
    "Umph! Damn, Girl, you so fine."

The boogeyman is real y'all
    even when she cries.

The boogeyman is real y'all
    even when she lies to apologize.

The boogeyman is real y'all
    when she falls short of every
    expectation, but says that she tries.

The boogeyman is real y'all.
The boogey man is real y'all.
The boogey man is real y'all.
And sometimes . . .
Just sometimes . . .
It lives in our own minds.

Nikesha Elise Williams

Pro-Life?!

I carried you.
For forty weeks...
I carried you.
Pushed you out of my body,
and latched you on to my breast;
I nursed you and nurtured you,
gave you golden milk to be fed.

I poured into you,
and watched you grow.
Denied myself so that you could flourish.
But,
you became the opposite of what I hoped.
One of the ones who think they came from thin
air,
and succeeded all on your own.

That because you have testes,
you have the right to tell me what I can or can't
do with my body.
When the truth of the matter is . . .
You became . . .
because of a fertilized egg from one of my
ovaries.
But now you legislate policy that is harmful to
me.

Lessons We Were Never Taught

Your mother.
Your grandmother.
Your daughter,
and your granddaughter.
All the women who came before you,
and the ones still to come after you.
We   are your lineage.
The ones who will carry the survival of your
legacy.

But all you want to do is stand on some biblical
moral high ground,
and spout false theology.
More concerned with fundraising for your
archaic political ideology.
Beating the drum of demagoguery,
training babes in your pedagogy
they don't even realize makes them
complicit in their own subjugation.

A party to their own oppression.
An accomplice to their own affliction.
And an active participant in the suppression of
their vote,
their voice,
and even their rights.

But, I guess being an adjacent proxy to power
makes it okay for the rest of us to lose the fight.
At least these are the lies you call "sacrifice"
in the name of being pro-life

But, can somebody please explain to me:

Nikesha Elise Williams

How you are pro-life and pro-gun?
Pro bump stocks on assault rifles.
                    Pro mass shootings and
                          school massacres.
                              Pro death
                              penalty.
                              Pro war.
                              Anti-welfare.
                              Anti-
                              healthcare.

     Anti-black and brown people without
specialized degrees from so called "shit hole"
countries. Anti-amnesty. Anti-womanhood,
and femininity. Opposed
    to everything
   you think
  may
  threaten
 your
patriarchy,
and self-
imposed
hegemony.

Please, tell me, "How does that make you
an advocate for those of us fortunate enough to
be living?"

Tell me,
if you're so "Pro-Life,"
How can you sit idly by

and support through your silence,
the extermination of an entire race through
police genocide?
Then have the audacity
to act like you care about my brown baby
getting here safely
to take his first cry?

Pardon me if I say, "You're full of it."
Because the truth of the matter is . . .
There are some things that just don't make
sense.

You're pro-life,
but it's okay if I die in labor —
or a few weeks later.
Because let's not forget,
our maternal death rates are worse than those
in less developed countries in South America,
Africa, or East Asia.

You want us to have babies
we were raped into conceiving,
incestuously coerced into producing,
and then kill the ones we love.
The ones we hold in our arms, rocking back
and forth, begging,
"Baby please,
 please,
  please,
keep on breathing."

What do you see when you look at me?

Nikesha Elise Williams

A woman?
A mother?
Or a descendant of slaves whose only role was
to keep on breeding?
To produce a crop of niggers you could keep
on beating.
The strange fruit it's okay for you to kill,
but it's against the law
if I withdraw
if you happen to discern
that there is another heart
inside of me beating.

Let's be real, you're not doing me no favors.
You don't care about my life,
                                            or my child.
You're neither benevolent or noble.
This shit here,   is all about
control.
To establish dominance and power in the one
area of expertise you will never be able to
behold.

Motherhood is a tribe.
A sorority of specific initiates.
It is not to be entered into lightly,
or forced upon those
who are telling you
                                  they're not ready.

And this is more than just a matter of money...
But while we're on the subject,
unless you're putting out for:

Lessons We Were Never Taught

       Daycare.
       Diapers.
       Formula.
       Food.
       Clothes.
       Shoes.
       Shelter.
       College.
       And Grad School.

You can miss me with all that talk.
Take that message on some elsewhere while you walk.
Because what we're not gon' do,
is act like any of this is simple.
Choices and regrets.
Decisions and memories you can't forget,
no matter how wide you smile
to show off your dimples.
So, let's cut the bullshit,
and pop these conservatively, populist,
political stances like pimples.

Tell me,
What do you see when you see my son?
What do you see when you see my daughter?
What do you see when you see my queer,
                      non binary,
                      gender
                      non-
                      conforming
                      mini-me

prancing, dancing, strutting, stunting,
studding down your street?
What do you see when I'm bowled over with a
big belly wondering if I will ever be able to
raise my child in peace?
This woman's work is not easy.

It's not as simple as picking sides such as pro-
life or pro-choice.
But you would know that if you ever bothered
to listen to a woman and really hear her voice.

    So.   Hear.   Me.   NOW.

It is neither my place nor yours to castigate
those who choose to abort.
Instead of separating church and state;
why don't you legislate your way out of my
vagina?
Do us all a favor and see your way out of my
uterus.
And for all you bandwagon bleeding hearts,
    We're not new this.
        We're true to this.

We see the scheme to get to the Supreme Court.
To go before the right-leaning,
stacked panel,
using unborn baby's lives as sport.
You say your beef is with the unjust decision of
Roe v. Wade.
But, uh, just so you know . . .
Overturning access and opportunity

won't get your womenfolk to fall in line and behave.
We are not your **Handmaid**.
We are women.

Red Blooded.
Heart Beating.
Self-affirming.
Life Giving.
Women!

We will use our voice,
and defend our choice.
It's not that we don't care,
               don't love,
               don't feel
Or we're so callous,
our only goal is to kill.

It is that we love so much,
care so deeply,
feel so completely . . .
We want to make sure we can give all of that to any child who we are ever graced to bring into being.

This is what it means to have options.
To decide.
To weigh the scales.
To choose for you — and for me — what is right.
This is what it means to support choice
and be   Pro-life!?

Nikesha Elise Williams

Mothers of Sorrow

I've crossed cities and states.
I've crossed countries.
I've crossed continents.
There was once and ocean between you and me.
There was once a mountain range standing between me and my destiny.
There was once
an arid desert standing between me,
and who I'm trying to be.

So, I set out   on the land that was
                         safer than the sea.

I was forced to leave   on the sea that was
                         safer than the land.

Torn from my home,
I was dragged across the only ground I've ever known.

But . . .
All the while . . .
All the while . . .
All the while . . .

Lessons We Were Never Taught

There was something inside of me.
Something bigger than me.
Something clinging to me.

A small hand wrapped up in mine.
Her three fingers held on to just one of mine.
His sweaty palm clasped itself,
and stuck to my skin.
And I still remember a time before his teeth came in.
Before her teeth came in.
Before their teeth came in.

When they clamped down and fed from my breast.
Gained essence,
      nutrients,
      purpose
      and life
from my chest.

So now as we walk on this rocky ground.
Tread carefully our steps in this caravan trying not to make a sound.
Cry out from the belly of a ship where we lay in our bowels . . .
No one hears us.
No one sees us.
No one   is concerned   about us.

They hear neither your whimpers nor my muffled sighs.

They pay no attention to my mellifluous
language
spat rapid fire in my   fear.
The tongues of my ancestors,
the spirits of my soul,
the God of my guidance is not here . . .
with me . . .
                                        anymore.

I am a foreigner in a stolen place.
An other who forced them to create race.
I am their burden and their proof,
of what happens when you take what does not
belong to you.
So, yeah, I crawled in and snuck my way
through,
to do the job that you didn't want to.

I was beaten and whipped,
                chained,
                hanged,
            and lynched …
And yet,
        I still made your food
into a comfort   for me.
Took the scraps from your table and turned
them into a national delicacy because:

I am the Earth.
I am the Earth.
I am the Earth.

Lessons We Were Never Taught

She is my mother,
and we are her daughters.
Fully built,
and equipped
to take the shit you give and turn it into sugar.

Until you began to take   what we birthed.
Tore from our arms,
pulled from our teats,
babies that still needed to be nursed.

You took our girls and our boys.
Our pride and our joy.
You took them and we wailed,
and from our gut,
all of our divine enlightenment bubbled up,
and we choked   on our own stuff.

We were suffocated.
We were asphyxiated . . .
By the loss of those three fingers holding on in
our hand.
That sweaty palm and sticky skin
that pressed through to touch and to feel our
inner man.

You took the men we reaped!
The boys whose secrets we dreamed to sleep.
The girls whose desires we put inside
ourselves and dared to believe.
It started in 1619!
And for the last 400 years it has been
happening every day,

every year since.

You abolish the trade
only to give it another name.
We suffer under Jim Crow,
become refugees of terror on a Great Migration North,
to where the winter does snow.
We become "civil,"
but you do us no favors by reinstating our rights . . .
Because our brown LatinX brothers and sisters
are still forced to take flight.
From the guns and the drugs you supplied,
To the land of opportunity you want us to sing
about with pride.

Well, pardon me if I take a knee.
Pardon us if we stand together linking arms in solidarity . . .
Because the same shit you did yesterday,
you do today.
Only it's under another name.
Another policy.
Another bullshit ass excuse for lacking basic human decency.

      Law. And. Order.

Allows you to empty your six shots
on my block
into a black body that perseverates from being
pumped with lead.

Lessons We Were Never Taught

You fill our prisons with moms and dads,
girls and boys,
dressed in swimsuits and armed with toys.
They see your lights and automatically know
to run,
or quake with dread.
Immigration is just a dog whistle for you to
fear-monger your base into a frenzy,
yelling at the hoards you created,
"Go back to your country
                      or off with your head."

But there is no wall too high,
          no ocean too deep,
          no mountain that can't be
          moved . . .
For us to get
what we came for . . .
Our children.

You may take their bodies,
but you will never get their souls.
You may stick them in steel cages,
and cover them with foil blankets but,

They will always be mine.
They will always be mine.
They will always be mine.

I will not sing a sad song.
I will not mourn in my grief.
I will not give you the satisfaction of seeing the
indignity of my undoing.

I am not a mother of sorrow.
I am a mother of rage.
I am a mother of anger.
Vengeance is mine
thus saith the mothers.
Don't think
you can take what I birth and think that I won't
consume you.
Drown you in my oceans,
Strand you in my deserts,
Leave you rescue-less
at the tips
of my highest peaks,
Until you return to me …
That   which you   did not   conceive.

The men.
The women.
The girls.
The boys.
Every black, and brown, and othered body
whose obsequious smiles are no longer here to
serve
YOU!

They belong to me.
They belong to me.
They belong to me.

I am their mother.
She is their mother.
We are their mothers.

Lessons We Were Never Taught

And nothing,
not even death,
            can keep us from them.

Nikesha Elise Williams

A Tribute to Men

I heard a poet say, "Nigga, you ain't shit!"
But what she was really saying was, "Nigga,
you *ain't*, shit."
And you're not a nigga either.
You're more than the labels and lies society's
laid on you.
More than the negative forces forced upon you.
More than the anachronistic anathema,
More than the stereotypical bullshit assigned to
you.

You don't have to ascribe to the lies meant to
oppress.
You don't have to only achieve to the stifling
ceiling limits of success.
Success is what you make it.
Goals are dreams with deadlines that you set.

Your abilities are determined by the creativity
of your mental capacity,
not some whack ass system forcing you to
learn chemistry and trigonometry.

So, you can pass a test
that was designed for you to come out less
than second best.
To give those who in-breed on corporate greed

Lessons We Were Never Taught

another reason to build a bed
for you to lay your head
behind bars,
and inside concrete walls.

The rich get richer on the backs of free prison labor.
The New Jim Crow;
makes moot the first half of the thirteenth amendment,
so you are no longer five fifths amended

They say race is a social construct.
Nothing more than lies we've made true,
put faith and belief into.
But, can someone please tell me how
we can dismantle the complex infrastructure
holding the construct together?

How do we address what is, but isn't?
How do we redress what was never intended?
How do we right the wrongs that prevented progress?
How do we fight the power,
the people we elected to Congress?

The ones who make the rules,
approve the contracts,
take the kick-backs after a slap of a hand and a pat on the back?
How do we get them to get their foot off of
your neck so you can stand up, stretch, and
maybe even flex a li'l bit?

Nikesha Elise Williams

Somebody please tell me so we can begin the egress.

Somebody.
Anybody.
Nobody.
No takers.
Well, then, I guess I'll digress.

Because there's more than "the man" second guessing your being.
Scheming on ways he can keep you from achieving.
Because even though it's hard to admit,
and I often want to circumvent
                        this next truth . . .
When it comes to keeping you from reaching your full potential,
I have to raise my hand and add myself to the problem by saying,   "Me Too."

I'm supposed to be part of your equation.
A teammate. A partner.
But what I received as my birth right
is the full experience of male emasculation.

My ancestors were breeders and yours were bucks,
brought together for clandestine connections
that taught us to fuck
                    but not love.

Lessons We Were Never Taught

I never learned how to be a whole half to your
whole half.
I learned to be whole and complete
even if that meant without you.
'Cause it don't matter what the rest of the
world says if I'm the first one to doubt you.
To take your accomplishments and turn them
into jokes.
Because the pain inside I cannot describe
teaches me to laugh to keep from crying . . .
When all you and me are doing is trying.

Trying to reverse the course set forth in our
DNA.
The double helix embedded with code that
says you can leave,
                        because I'll stay.
The fucked-up concept born of the construct
that made us identify with titles and customs
that didn't belong to us.
So that our history could be white-washed,
gentrified, and polished up in a shiny, white,
Sphinx bust.
So that we'd forget we held the original keys to
all the kingdoms.

We created: Literature and Art.
                    Revolutionized Architecture.
And we're so wildly off the spectrum
that we had to be conditioned to submit,
and to our detriment
                        that mentality still persists.

It shows up in how we relate to one another.
The man in you and the woman in me always searching,
but never able to find what's right in front of our eyes.

You're looking for the Queen in me,
just like I'm looking for the King in you.
Not   the God in you.
Because that's too much for me to ask of you . . .
For you to be my God
When you have your own burdens
        to bear,
        to sort through,
  and some to carry around.

I know that heavy is the head that wears the crown.
Weary are the shoulders that hold up the world.
Broken is the back costumed in lack
In sambo.
In coon.
In a blackfaced jiggaboo.

You   are nobody's caricature.
No archetype of a stereotype.
A playing on of the high-brow for low-brow entertainment.
Cake walking in couture and not even getting paid for it.

Lessons We Were Never Taught

You've been hooping on hope,
balling on backboard dreams,
batting ten thousand just to get to the major leagues.
All because they applaud of what you can do for them.
Not because you learned how to walk on water
    when they didn't even want to teach
    you how to swim.

Excellence is your inheritance.
Your birthright.
The rights you never lost,
despite the middle passages crossed.
The reparations never paid,
the bricks you laid on chain gangs,
when arrested for loitering and whistling.

So,   Black Man:
Forget the lies applied when they can't even
decipher the meaning of your cries.
Instead arrest yourself to a cypher.
Handcuff your being to your own dreams,
and make miracles and magic just from the
unique way you see things.

And when it comes to me:
Be patient with my growth,
because our revolution depends on our own
individual evolution;
both mine and yours.

Nikesha Elise Williams

We'll be unstoppable to:
        chart the course,
        plot the path,
        direct the steps,
        introduce the new world order,
and then jet set to what's next.

This is what's possible for you,
                and me too.
What we are capable of producing from the
fruit of our labor,
the work of our hands
the endless imagination of woman and man

So, when the world tells you, "Nigga, you ain't
shit."
Just nod your head and say, "I know."

Because you have thirty-thousand ancestors
holding you down.
And a whole host of angels ready to strap up
and hound,
The devils and demons that want to keep you
from being great;
To stifle what's inside you so you never
graduate . . .

From the prisons they erected,
and the beds that they made.
The tests designed for you to fail,
so you would never excel

beyond the tiny parameters for you to fit into
their world,
    which is your own personal hell.

But there is divine light inside you.
Formed in the image of the creator,
you were called to be greater . . .
By just being who you are:
The warrior.
The father.
The provider.
The comforter.
The commander in chief of your own
destiny. . .

This
    is who you were meant to be.
More than a conqueror; you were born to win.
And *this* I tell you
    is a tribute
        to Black men.

Nikesha Elise Williams

Malcolm and June

What is a riot,
but a revolution without the prism of
privilege?

It is the voice of the oppressed
expressed in fiery shouts of rage.
Because the only way we can get people to
engage,
is to become exactly who they think we are.
Fulfilling a prophecy we never had about
ourselves.
Playing into pre-written scripts
that cite lack of intelligence,
and highlight our strength
                as a means to justify racist ends.

Just because you see muscles ripple in our
back,
and tendons gleam beneath our skin,
does not mean that there aren't thoughts
processed by the computer held within.
Beneath the fleshy folds
of our frontal lobe
lies the desire for freedom.
The yearning to be more than just one thing.
But the world has a way of crushing our ideas
before we can dream,

a way of silencing our voices before we ever
get it into our head to scream.

So, by the time we come out of the meek,
and docile act;
there is no time left for outsiders to react.
Because what we recognize as the bleeding
heart of pain . . .
Is assumed to be a rebellion . . .
Against what   they cannot say.

So, I ask you,

"What is a riot, but a guerrilla war waged
against colonizers who specialize in
Columbising everything that was never lost
they claimed they found?

Stealing the sights and sounds, music, food
and even the way we sing our
ShoooooooBeeeeeeeeeDoooooooBeeeeeDooos.

What is a revolution?

Is it not warfare to determine whether
Darwin's theory of evolution still stands?
Whether the survival of the fittest is found in
the best black, white, brown, or other kind of
man?

Is it not the reason Israel fought Egypt, Assyria,
and Babylon?

Nikesha Elise Williams

The reason God's children have no place in the
world to belong.
The reason Alexander the Great and
Constantine became known as great invaders.
The reason Portugal, Britain, France, and Spain
became great raiders.

Stealing natural resources that can never be
replaced.
Thirteen million souls strong.
Thirteen million souls gone
in the business that created race.

Known for "discovering" what was already
there,
laying claim to what already had a name,
establishing superiority among a people who
never knew inferiority.
Then they wonder why bondage didn't fit.
Why against their dominance we resist.
Why their power we don't respect.
And why in anything we do we say, "We the
best!"

We don't need a revolution,
when we've already found the solution,
to end our tears at their expense.
To stop our pain without false pretense,
and to break free of social constructs
that were never meant for us.

But, how, can we resolve to evolve beyond ablution,
when we don't even have a stake in our own constitution?
So, what is the point of a revolution?

Through their eyes it will just be seen as another desperate cry for help.
Not connected to any other event.
An apparent
         disparate
                  moment
That will soon be forgotten.

I guess that's why we always have on reserve
the evocative word
to create and conjure . . .
images of destructive violence
beyond the rapture . . .
the Riot.

But what is a riot, but an unrevered insurrection?

The steps back we voluntarily take to course correct and begin to go in the right direction.
The lessons in all the ways that are rightfully wrong just to get attention.
Because we've run out of cares,
                damns,
             and fucks to give.
If going backwards means we'll find the route that leads us to live.

The path that promises more than slaveholding
ancestors ever did.

Beyond the call for reparations,
that's become a presidential play in
patronization.
We have no more use for forty acres and a
mule,
but we can always be repaid with equal
schools.
Not the discarded leftovers left over after white
flight,
but the ones where academics matter more
than sports.
Books are current.
The arts are valued.
And the ugly stains of my black history
don't suffer an erasure
to protect white tears and feelings like our pain
doesn't matter.

In this school where we educate the next
generation,
they will learn the difference between critical
theory and indoctrination.
So, whenever they are faced with an equation
     or question . . . like
"What is the difference between a riot and a
revolution?"
They can stand flat footed and firm in their
answer and say:

"What is a riot or revolution but a response to a raised black fist in the air.
The silent yet demonstrative protest.
That makes those wonder if they should second guess:
    The evolution of the sit-in.
    The maturation of the march.
    And the increased sophistication of the protest picket sign."

Our revolutions were spawned from riots that left:
    An indelible mark.
    A lasting impression.
    And a permanent tattoo that says we will no longer accept   hostile transgressions,
                    overt racism,
    or workplace micro-aggressions.

We have come to claim all of our unalienable rights:
                Life.
                Liberty.
        And the Pursuit of Happiness . . .
Even if that means we have to fight.

Too many are sacrificing their lives for the greater good only to never get it.
Their bloated bodies flashed on TV screens without care for their humanity.
Or upon arrival they're ushered through immigration and housed in cages,
yet none of us are supposed to think

that these high security brick and mortar
facilities are the new plantation.
We are no longer accepting the convincings of
alternative facts.
We don't buy into social media propaganda
disguised as marketing e-blasts.
We're not here for fixed elections or hanging
chads.

We're here to go:
                Toe to Toe,
                Round for Round,
                Swing for Swing,
and we won't back down.

Because come hell or high water . . .
Riot or revolution . . .
Call it whatever you want,
just make sure there's no confusion.

We are Here
in spite of what you seem to believe is our
perceived disadvantaged lack.
Our very survival

                is a revolutionary act.

Lessons We Were Never Taught

Baldwin

This   is an ode to self.
An ode to me.
An ode to be . . .
Freely and comfortably
who I've been called and created to be,
see,
and see succeed in this world.

This   is an ode to self.
Not an ode to anyone else.
Not a promise to live selfless,
because for those whom I do . . .
they don't even know how to appreciate.
I either damn near die trying to keep them,
or I lose them to a celestial realm
which only adds another crack to my porcelain
body armor that refuses to break.

I am no longer in the habit to make a difference
to the damned if I do, damned if I don't ilk.
I will no longer hold on to this guilt.
I'm not in the headspace to add any more
shame,
    any more blame,
        any more baggage,
            any more bricks to this wall of
            judgement we built.

Today I own my part in condemning
myself
     for being   myself.
For convicting myself.
For refusing to contort and conform into the
mold of anyone else.
I will take my portion of my soul concession
and mend my spirit.
This   is my confession:

"I played a part in neglecting me.
I had a hand in being second.
You see,
I thought if I put everyone first —
especially the one I birthed —
eventually someone would do the same for
me."

But, a humble back breaks,
the selfless servant gets tired,
and the forgotten bride gets wired to realize
that the servant's heart is never coming back
around in the form of another.
No one else will love or treat you like your
mother.

So, Honey, take what you know and begin to
serve yourself.
Pour not from an empty cup,
but fill yourself up,
with the love and devotion you so freely give.
Invest, digest, and consume more than your
daily dose of Jesus wept.

Lessons We Were Never Taught

Fill up with the Most High,
but don't forget to fill up with you.
We were created whole and complete,
never meant to run on empty.

Learning always.
Evolving always
Growing in days, and weeks, and points.
So, Babygirl, pump some life into those joints . . .
by just doing the the shit you love.

Who cares what others say?
This is not for them, and today is not their day.

This   is an ode to self
Not for anyone else.
An ode giving me permission,
to finally be selfish,
with myself.
To do for me.
To tend to me.
To bend for me.
To be uncompromising.

Steadfast and immovable.
Obstinate, stubborn, intransigent, and
intractable.
Daring anyone who would ever feel some kind
of way to leave,
because today . . .
I'm just gon' breathe.

Breathing on the outskirts;
a true introvert.
It's not that I'm stand offish;
I'm just introspective.
Trying to get the right perspective,
to have clarity and foresight,
instead of regrets and hindsight.
I'm trying to have insight instead of plain old sight.

What I can see may not always be for me.
I need to evince beyond my midnight dreams.
So,
    I'm looking in,
        navel gazing
            and digging deep
                to find that spirit of peace.
The one that births and manifests stars and seas,
or maybe poems and plays
                at the very least.

I'm trying to do more than scratch the surface.
I'm planning on living on purpose.
Casting aside what is worthless,
armoring up with what pisses you off because I deserve it.

I Am   my most prized possession.
And I'm finally mature enough to defend and protect it.

Lessons We Were Never Taught

I have grown up.
Given up.
Started over.
And still couldn't find which way was up.
Because first,   I had to find me.

I had to learn what I like and love.
Hell, what even gets on my own damn nerves.
I had to look in the mirror and make peace
with the past.
And when I find pieces of my history bubbling
up in the present,
I have to give myself a warning and say,
"Not so fast."

Hold on to what you claimed.
Don't be so quick to gearshift because someone
else says your soul search for self is lame.
Nothing about me is a mistake.
Nothing about me needs to be fixed or
changed.
> At least not in the flesh
> This ugly robe is as useless as a vest.
> And I don't mean to offend,
> there's just a few more things I need
> to get off my chest.

I am on a quest.
A search to find and be at God's best.
That means there are some things,
some people,
some places,
and some behaviors,

that will have to get left.

I'm taking everything and nothing less
And sorry,
I'm not sorry if what you think I look like is
such a mess.
I don't give a damn about your looks or
concerns, thoughts, assumptions, judgements
or even your guess.

I am here to make manifest . . .
Every metaphor about a matador who taunts
with red cloth.
Pretending to be ready to ride a bull,
but doesn't want to sacrifice when he
has to pay the cost,
and is tossed and thrown off
by an indomitable animal that cannot be
tamed.

I Am   that bull.
                        Puffing.
                        Snorting.
                        Roaring,
                        Raging.
Ready to break out, break free, and live
selfishly.
Multiplying exponentially,
in order to revive a spark in me;
that encourages my inner self to live
authentically.
Instead of living expectantly,
I will live exceptionally.

No matter how much the world demands,
instead of jumping at every beck and call,
I make commands.
Give orders and instruct myself to start by
loving me,
look in the reflecting glass and say, "Damn," at
everything I see.
So, when I proclaim, "I'm only in this for me."
All the naysayers and haters around me will
know I mean that shit unequivocally.

I'm on my way to a destination and it starts
with a journey . . .
Into unknown, unpeeled territory.
Into wild blossoms of field flowers of my
deepest darkest secrets.
I'm tending to my garden and planting seeds
for a season.

When I reap, I will be more than on the way to
mend.
I will have reached the end of my fucks to give.
Because I'm on a mission to live
for every piece,
and every part,
of every woman
who was ever told to put her soul on a shelf.
This is your lifeline.
The one you need at your beck and call.
I AM
                      your help.

Nikesha Elise Williams

For once . . .
Balance you first among everything
     and   everyone else.
Start right now.
Looking in the mirror.
Repeat after me.
"*This*   is an ode to self."

Lessons We Were Never Taught

Mylen

I knew you were mine from the moment I
looked at you.
And not just because you have my eyes,
which you do.
But because I knew deep down in my soul that
for you I would die.
And just so you know, your mommy is scared
of death.
My faith has helped ease it,
but it's still not a trip I'm looking forward to
make.

But for you . . .

I would sacrifice.
Lay down my very life,
and head to the murky abyss.
Greet Hades in purgatory,
or Jesus in jubilee,
depending upon the circumstances of how the
end of my life came to be.
Because if someone hurt you and changed
your future by their actions,
I would no longer be responsible nor feel the
need to repent for my lethal reaction.
I would happily greet hell
And this is what I'm trying to tell . . .

For you,   I would lose my religion.
For you,   I would do everything that scares
           me.
If that means keeping you safe,
protecting you from harm's way,
I'd greet my end with a smize,
and look forward to what we all will go
through and know it will be a beautiful
surprise.

And I don't mean to spend so long explaining
the extremes of my love,
but you should know by now that mommy can
be a bit dramatic.
And all my shucking, and jiving, and acting a
fool in the name of my art,
is now evidenced in you who only wants to be
called cool, instead of handsome or smart.

But son you are all of those things:
                Cute.
                Handsome.
                Smart.
                Cool.
All of the delicate descriptors I can conjure
apply to you . . . my favorite boy
Because you   are my life's greatest joy.

From the moment I knew you existed inside
me . . .
My chest began to swell,
and my heart began to heave,
because I knew decidedly

Lessons We Were Never Taught

that from by your side I'd never want to leave.

I loved you the most because I knew you from your beginning.
You on the inside and me on the out.
But now that you're here on this Earth
    walking,
        running,
           and biking about.
I have to confront the reality,
that you're growing up.

Not a baby anymore.
A big boy with thoughts and opinions all his own.
Seeing you like this now gives me a glimpse of who you'll be as a man:
        Determined.
        Proud.
        Strong.
        Confident.
        Arrogant.
In tune with your sensitivities,
and certain about your proclivities —
your bent toward the finer, nicer things in life.

Able to cope with strife and struggle,
and because you get it from your daddy you'll definitely know how to hustle.
How to make a million dollars out of fifteen cents.
Never wavering from what you know to be true,

because you are the proof,
the evidence.
With air, water, and a new day as your motivation,
there will be nothing you can't conquer as your occupation.

And it is not my intent to put my delayed dreams on you.
Because I want you to see me and daddy work with you by our side.
To let you know that you can do whatever you want,
and don't ever have to make up for what you assume to be our compromise.

You were made in love and gifted to us.
The one whose name means gracious or merciful.
Dear one or gift of God.
But whatever variation you choose,
know that it's all true;
even the definition that you are the center of the plain.
You anchored me to the earth,
and became my sun.
Made me realize my life is now bigger than just me,
and that there was another whose needs,
                    whose wants,
                    whose desires
mattered more than mine.

That's why I always try to take the time to
indulge you.
Be it walks or talks.
Bike rides or playing at the park.
Or you messing with me because it's your
favorite past time,
or watching *Minions* on TV for the hundredth
thousandth time.

I will be your rock
and you my feather.
Able to fly off without fear
because I will always be here . . .
For you to return when you need.
In a way,
        I am your creed.
Giving you credence to do in this world
whatever you like,
because giving you life has already been your
greatest gift to me.
So, I want you to be all that you can be.

And while you'll never join the Army,
because daddy's a Marine,
You'll uphold the mantra:
    The few.
    The proud.
    The bold.
Creating.
Innovating.
And running industries still untold.

No matter what you do,

Nikesha Elise Williams

I'll always be proud of you.
You don't have to ask
I've always got your back.
And your front,
because your grandma didn't raise no fool or no punk.

The lineage from which you descended on
both sides of your birth,
is one that is ruefully and wholly connected to
the Earth.
One that reveres the heavens,
and respects the people.
One that doesn't bend to any whim,
or bow to any them,
because as a black man you can and will
always proclaim,
        "I AM a MAN."
And they better call you by your name.

Mylen.

You are my life's greatest joy.
My favorite boy.
I hope this note grows with you as you age,
and when I'm no longer here it becomes your
favorite friend;
more than an epitaph or adage.

You know in my own words.
From my own hand,
and my own mouth,
the day you were born

Lessons We Were Never Taught

is the day my life changed.

I would never trade anything to not have you.
I will love you always.
Like Stevie wonder sang,
You ain't gotta worry 'bout a thang.

I'm so glad that each day with you is never the same.
You teach me as much as I teach you:
    Patience.
    Kindness.
  And the meaning of true love.

We are unconditionally bonded.
Tested, tried, and made for each other.
From our four-hour naps,
to the cock of our head
the looks we make when we slide our eyes to the side,
or even the way we sigh.

With you I see so much of me.
And I am glad that your humanity is developing beautifully.
You are affirmed when just your name is mentioned,
there is nothing anyone can do to take away your swag, shine, or attention.

So always remember,

Dear Mylen,

Nikesha Elise Williams

My baby boy.
No matter what anybody says, does, or tries to convince you of in this world,
Always know, you are my life's greatest joy.

Lessons We Were Never Taught

Maya

The water we carry.
The bowls we hold.
The drinks we never swallow.
The loads we never wash or fold.
The water from our eyes.
The tears we never want to cry.
The water from our bodies.
The life's worth of liquid that makes us next to Godly.

We bear the bullion of family burdens.
We dig the wells where secrets are shed.
On the beds where death comes to greet us,
is where we learn the history mother never intended to meet us.

In keeping the lineage of which we were born into hidden,
we can walk this life in full oblivion.
Confident that our past has no bearing,
and our future is wide open.
Believing in our power to do and be anything,
and nothing rising up against us can't be bent bowed, bound, or broken.

But there comes a time when our invincible spirit is tested.
There comes a time, that by no fault of our own, we are bested.

As we lick our wounds, and heal our pride,
Repair our wounded egos, and make a choice . . . do we decide:
    To stay or go.
    To fight or flee.
    Remaining where we are is not an option,
    but it's still so damn hard to leave.

To put one foot in front of another
To roll through my metatarsal,
and make my toes set the path for my ankles to follow.

On uncharted courses and through unmapped waters
    I go as a hostage to my truth.
A prisoner of my intrinsic need to find proof.
The answers my ancestors found.
The secrets they sent me with as I made my way through the birth canal.

It is time for me to return home.
To return to them.
To pay tribute for what they bought paid and slaved for,
the forced servitude and genocide they refused to abide.

Lessons We Were Never Taught

So, in the new world at Igbos Landing they chose mass suicide,
instead of a life of "Yassa, Massa I."

I am here to bring water to their well.
I go unwillingly but dutifully.
Being obedient to the call beating within me
I follow the talking drum.
Walking back through the door of no return on the journey that is the destination.
I am here to submit for their consideration,
this humble bowl I picked up when I set down my load . . .
          It is my libation.

I am here to bring water to the well.
To pour out my offering to my eggun who live in paradise beyond the veil.
Because there is nothing like the wisdom of old people.
The audacity of their sagacity gives me the knowledge I need to lay hold of everything within my capacity.
 So, I sit at their feet as they tell me,

"Daughter, this is your legacy
To build what we could not.
To love those whom we could not.
To take the opportunities that we had not.
And to run further than our bare feet could carry us,
because our weary bones, muscles, and tendons had knots."

"You are not, a not
You are a no more."

They speak in parables to me about all the life I
have in store.
In allegory they tell me that because they came
before,
they set me on a course so that my life's work
would not be doing chores.
They labored so I would have the option to be
an entrepreneur.
And in metaphor they paralleled the
comparisons of yester, yonder, and yore.

They are the personification of truth.
My ancestors.
My hedge of protection upon which I was
called forth.
        Birthed.
               And brought into this world.

I stand on their shoulders,
and live in their legacy.
I am the simile they liked as much as they
loved the comfort of resting in peace.

So, I am here at their well
Sitting before their stones.
Drawing from them again;
before I drown in the pools of sin
that looks like every woman's tall, dark, and
handsome feckless temptation.

I am here at their well.
Sitting at their feet.
Drawing from them again,
wisdom against the recklessness of my
carelessness.
Decisions I knew would be a mistake before I
even got in.

Into that career that was only a job.
Into that relationship that was only a fling.
Into this motherhood when I should have been
more proactive to wrap up his thing.
Or more pro-choice to do what some consider
unconscionable.
Or more pro-life that I should have had a
shotgun wedding and became a selfish wife.

I am here at their well.
Longing to gaze upon their faces,
and draw directly from their lips.
Rebuke and admiration for every flight of
fancy they didn't have time to imagine
let alone to ego trip.

I am here to draw wisdom from their well of
living water.
I am here for knowledge and learning.
Tutelage and mentorship.
Direction and clarity.
All the things I can carry back from whence I
came.

The invisible force
and the impenetrable shield no one can see but
I know is there,
that gives me courage to stand up and defend
our good name.

I am the Little Dipper and they are the
drinking gourd.
I follow the path they left for me written across
the hosts of starry skies.
On moonless nighs we get into intense
conversations.
They lead me through the clarification of
constellations . . .
And how they apply to my life.
They explain to me that beyond burden and
strife,
I am the one they sent to cut the coils of
bondage with a knife.

Sawing through brokenness.
Hacking through feelings of inadequacy.
Slashing through doubt.
Carving through fear.
And cleaving away at the gripping whispers
that say I am unworthy.

They gladly watch as I loose what lived deep
inside our ancestral village.
The matriarchal rituals that got lost when all
we were allowed to rely on were old negro
spirituals.

Lessons We Were Never Taught

Depending on a blue-eyed Jesus we didn't
know to get us through agricultural hell.

They watch with smiles as I loose us from the
trauma whipped in my genetic code.
Breaking the chains,
ripping the shackles,
and splitting the neck collars that should have
never been a part of my fleshy domicile;
let alone my bodily abode.

I came bringing water to their well.
Searching for guidance I hear the voice living
inside us that says,

"Daughter it is time to ring the bell.
It is time for you to announce,
     We are free at last.
     We are free at last.
     We are free . . .
                            At last."

"To do the one thing we never thought.
To take back what should have never been
caught.
To reclaim and up charge for what should have
never been bought.
And make the leery searcher weary for the
dark human cargo he sought."

"Bring your water.
Pour out your devotion.
Now take up your bowl,

and return to your land away from our ocean.
Carry this notion in your heart:"

"We live in you.
There is never a time when you can't look
inside and see us.
Stand in the mirror,
open your memory,
reach back and be us."

"Like you,
we have carried you;
the eggs in our ovaries.
And you have carried us,
in your spirit and psyche.
So, carry our water.
Hold our bowls.
Swallow our drinks.
And make sure our loads are washed to fold."

"Let the water run from your eyes.
Let the tears out and cry.
Let the offering come out of your body.
So that you always remember this life's worth
of liquid is what makes you Godly."

"It is within you.
Our divine energy.
A synergy built up from generation to
generation to generation.
And now it is your occupation
to harness the efficacy in your vitality.
The fidelity in your faculties.

And the possibilities and potentialities in all of your manifested opportunities."

"Daughter this is your calling.
This is your duty and your destiny.
Listen closely to me.
Take us with you into the future.
Where we
will all
be free."

Nikesha Elise Williams

Joy

I can't write any more poems of pain.
No more words where the ink runs with my
tear stains.
I can tell no more tales of those who left or
worse yet,
         never came.
I can spin no more stories urging,
                 persisting,
                 insisting
that you speak their names.

There is more to me than being a harbinger for
the world's,
    my country's,
    my people's grief.
There is more to this black female existence
than to tuck away and reconcile
every person,
      race,
      and culture that approaches me as a
      thief.

Because the truth is . . .
There would be no you without me.
No one to look up to.
No one to keep your secrets.
No one to wipe your tears.

Lessons We Were Never Taught

No one to swallow your fears.

We set the standard.
The bar.
We move the measuring stick;
                        And the culture.
We're on to the next when you're still feeding
off our old shit you fucking vultures.

I say that with a smile.
Imitation is the sincerest form of flattery,
and try as you might your mimicry is nowhere
near to being an exact copy.
Let alone something you could rip off and call
your own.

That's why we feel joy in spite of you.
Can laugh, smile, and roll our eyes despite the
dirt you do.
We were force fed verses to keep us in line,
to keep us looking toward a future hoping.
     You know how it goes,
      "Weeping lasts for a night,
      but joy cometh in the morning."

But joy is what,
      when,
      whom,
      and wherever I want it.

Joy is sewing buttons on ice cream.
Joy is making my man scream.
Joy is watching my baby take his first step.

Joy is knowing my heart can beat and leap and
I too deserve to be swept . . .
                        up off my feet by frivolities.
I can laze my days away and no ones
    Stopping me.
    Checking me.
    Blocking me.
    Watching me.
    Hawking me.
    Gawking at me.
Wondering why I got the right to feel so damn free.

Well,
I'll tell you why.
I earned it.

I earned the peace that surpasses all understanding.
I earned the right to not be questioned.
I earned the right to be taken at my word.
I earned the right to be paid what I deserve.
I earned the right to respect.
I earned the right to dream.
To believe in the fruit of life even if it's not always seen.
I earned the right to a peaceful existence,
even if I do inherit one of pain and violence.
I earned everything you see,
but most of all I've earned the right to be fully and wholly me.

No sacrifice.

Lessons We Were Never Taught

No compromise.
No pieces to compartmentalize.
Just   Awesomeness.

Someone you esteem and greet with reverence.
And if you wanna get a li'l hood,
just say I'm that bitch.
Because however you flip it, spin it, or reverse it,
the truth of the matter is
we've always been something majestic.
Something to behold.
And never to be played,
                toyed
                        or trifled with.
Because at the end of the day we are the ones
you want to ride with.

Loyal to a fault.
Loving even after the heart stops.
That is what we're made of.
                Love.
                Peace.
                Joy.

All the ingredients everyone tried to take from us.
The intrinsic and esoteric accoutrements we were supposed to forget we had so that they could break us.

But we didn't forget.
And we couldn't be broke.

Nikesha Elise Williams

We don't need to stay woke,
you just need to wake up.
And once you do try your damndest to catch us,
because we've got joy, peace, and love feeding us.

This divine and Holy Trinity is our orisha.
This life we have on the inside . . .
you can never come between us.

So, you can run tell dat,
or keep it to yourself.
It really doesn't matter
if it's between you and nobody else.
Because I'm about to take off.
Mount up.
And harness the power of wings.

This   is joy
that keeps me lifted flying amongst celestial felicity.
This   is joy
that keeps me glad in my tidings.
This   is joy
that keeps me good, and never in mourning.
This   is joy
when I lift up ev'ry voice and sing.
This   is joy
until Earth and heaven ring.
This   is joy
ringing with all my sisters' harmonies.
This   is joy.

Lessons We Were Never Taught

So, "Wake up."
It is a new dawn.
A new day.
A new good feeling.
It is morning, Queens!

Acknowledgements

I began writing poetry as a pre-teen. It was a way for me to express myself and cope with the drama of my life at the time.

The practice stayed with me as I got older. When I was young, I wrote poems daily. However, as I got older the time with my journal became few and far between, and there were some months, some years, I went without writing any poems at all.

That all changed within the last two to three years. My TEDx talk, "Representation Matters" begins with a poem and is infused with poetry throughout. That poem is "Nina."

The same year I did both of my TEDx talks, I was invited to a gathering of writers and poets to use our literary art form to address the mass shooting at Marjory Stoneman Douglas High School in Parkland, Florida. That piece entitled, "National Anthem," (not included in this collection) was a spark that brought me back to poetry.

At the end of 2018, I was asked by an artist to write something relating to one of his art works. I did and in January of 2019 I performed that piece, "Mothers of Sorrow."

That piece didn't necessarily go viral, but it was well-received on the internet and the book of faces and was another spark to my fuse.

I began to muse with my therapist about what to do with the work, and she helped bring me back to my original dream.

At 18, I said I wanted to write and choreograph musicals.

This book and the accompanying one-woman show is the manifestation of all the old me wished and wanted for; and I have several people to thank for that.

First and foremost, Jesus, for my talent.

Keri Foster for arranging the, Verse Versus, showcase after Parkland.

Thony Aiuppy and Hope McMath for creating a space for "Mothers of Sorrow" to live (in both artwork and words.)

Erin Kendrick, your show, *Her Own Things*, and helping you on your BAM chapter set the stage for "Ntozake," to be born.

Stephanie Jones, thank you for always making me do the work and dig deep.

Nordica and Toya, our Christmas get together and conversation in 2018 led to the title of this work, and the collection as a whole. I hope you both feel seen and heard.

And to you, reader, I hope you enjoy the collection, and if you saw the show that goes with this collection, thank you. Immensely. From the bottom of my heart. This is truly scary for me; stepping into the fullness of everything I've ever said I wanted to be. But it is also deeply fulfilling, and I am forever

grateful, and forever indebted to you readers, friends, colleagues, ancestors, and Spirit of the Living God.
    Thank you.

Sincerely,

Nikesha Elise Williams

About the Author

Nikesha Elise Williams is a two-time Emmy award winning news producer and award-winning author.

She was born and raised in Chicago, Illinois, and attended The Florida State University where she graduated with a B.S. in Communication: Mass Media Studies and Honors English Creative Writing.

Nikesha's debut novel, *Four Women*, was awarded the 2018 Florida Authors and Publishers Association President's Award in the category of Adult Contemporary/Literary Fiction. *Four Women*, was also recognized by the National Association of Black Journalists as an Outstanding Literary Work.

Nikesha is a full time writer and writing coach and has freelanced for several publications including ESSENCE, VOX, Very Smart Brothas, and Shadow and Act.

Nikesha lives in Jacksonville, Florida, but you can always find her online at newwrites.com, Facebook.com/NikeshaElise

or @Nikesha_Elise on Twitter and Instagram.

www.ingramcontent.com/pod-product-compliance
Lightning Source LLC
Chambersburg PA
CBHW030327080526
44584CB00012B/746